The Atlas of the Seven Continents™

SOUTH AMERICA

Wendy Vierow

The Rosen Publishing Group's
PowerKids Press™
New York

For Chris, who loves atlases

Published in 2004 by The Rosen Publishing Group, Inc.
29 East 21st Street, New York, NY 10010

First Edition

Editor: Frances E. Ruffin
Book Design: Maria E. Melendez
Layout Design: Eric DePalo

Photo Credits: Cover and title page, Map of South America © Earth Observatory/NASA; p. 5 (bottom maps) illustrated by Maria Melendez; p. 7 © 2001 Todd Marshall; p. 9 (map symbols), p. 15 (map of South America) illustrated by Eric DePalo; pp. 9, 11, 13, 17 (map of South America), 19 (left maps), 21 (left maps) © GeoAtlas; p.11 (left maps) © Jacques Descloitres/NASA; p. 17 (Spider Monkey) © Tom Brakefield/CORBIS; p. 17 (Llama) © Blaine Harrington III/CORBIS; p. 17 (Sea Turtle) © Stephen Frink/CORBIS; p. 17 (Wild Orchids) © Galen Rowell/CORBIS; p. 19 (Assembling Aircraft) © John Madere/CORBIS; pp. 19 (Farmer), (Art Student) © Pablo Corral V/CORBIS; p. 21 (Young Girls in Canoe) © Kevin Schafer/CORBIS; pp. 21 (Ecuadorian Boys), (Young Dancer) © Pablo Corral V/CORBIS.

Vierow, Wendy.
South America / Wendy Vierow.— 1st ed.
    p. cm. — (The atlas of the seven continents)
Includes bibliographical references and index.
ISBN 0-8239-6693-3 (library binding)
1. South America—Geography—Juvenile literature. 2. South America—Maps for children. I. Title.
F2208.5 .V54 2004
918–dc21
                    2002156295

Manufactured in the United States of America

Contents

Earth's Continents and Oceans

Of Earth's seven continents, South America is the fourth largest after Asia, Africa, and North America. A continent is a large body of land. Earth's other continents are Antarctica, Australia, and Europe. South America is bordered by the Atlantic Ocean to the east and the Pacific Ocean to the west. The Arctic and Indian Oceans are Earth's other two oceans. Scientists think that, more than 200 million years ago, there was one giant continent called Pangaea, which was surrounded by one huge ocean called Panthalassa. Over time Pangaea broke into smaller continents. Even today the continents are moving. Scientists think that continents move because plates, or pieces of land, move below Earth's surface. These plates float on the partly melted rock deep inside Earth. When plates move, they cause changes on Earth's surface. Movements of Earth's plates can create mountains. The movements may also cause **earthquakes** and form volcanoes. The Andes Mountains contain active volcanoes and have many earthquakes. These mountains run from Venezuela along South America's west coast to the southern tip of Argentina.

Arctic Ocean

North America

Atlantic Ocean

Europe

Asia

Pacific Ocean

South America

Africa

Indian Ocean

Australia

Antarctica

PANGAEA

Equator

PERMIAN
286-245 million years ago

Equator

TRIASSIC
245-208 million years ago

Equator

JURASSIC
208-144 million years ago

Top: *This photo of Earth was taken high in space. Above and right: These maps show how the continent of Pangaea might have broken up into smaller continents. South America is shown in red.*

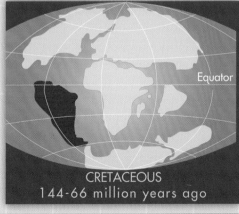

Equator

CRETACEOUS
144-66 million years ago

NORTH AMERICA

EUROPE ASIA

AFRICA

Equator

SOUTH AMERICA

AUSTRALIA

ANTARCTICA

PRESENT DAY
From 66 million years ago

South America Long Ago

The Mesozoic **era**, or Age of Dinosaurs, lasted from about 245 million to 66 million years ago. Scientists study fossils, the hardened remains of dead animals and plants, to learn about animals and plants that lived in that time. During the Mesozoic era in South America, *Opthalmosaurus*, a reptile that looked like a porpoise with huge eyes, searched for fish in the sea. Also in the water hunting for fish to eat was another reptile, *Metriorhynchus*, which was 10 feet (3 m) in length and looked like a crocodile. Diving for fish from the air was *Anhanguera*, a flying reptile that measured 13 feet (4 m) from wing to wing. On the ground was *Herrerasaurus*, a 13-foot-long (4-m-long) meat-eating dinosaur with sharp claws, which dined on reptiles and other dinosaurs. A plant-eating dinosaur called *Riojasaurus* measured 30 feet (9 m) long and was able to reach high branches by standing on its hind legs. Plants of the Mesozoic era included ginkgo trees and conifers, or trees with cones. Cycads, or trees that looked like palms or ferns, and the first flowering plants in South America also grew in during the Mesozoic era.

Tropeognathus was a pterosaur, or flying reptile, that flew high in the skies above South America from about 122 million to 112 million years ago. Tropeognathus had a wingspan of about 20 feet (6 m) and a skull that was 2 feet (67 cm) long and filled with many sharp teeth. Tropeognathus was a meat eater that dove down to a river or lake and snatched fish that swam near the surface of the water.

How to Read a Map

An atlas contains different kinds of maps. Maps have special features that make them easier to read. A map's title tells what the map shows. Often the title is located in the map key, or legend. The map key or legend explains the meaning of **symbols** on a map.

The map scale shows how the size of a map compares to the actual size of a place. A compass rose or north pointer shows directions on a map. The four main directions are north, south, east, and west. Latitude and longitude lines also show directions. Latitude lines run from east to west, and longitude lines run from north to south. The equator is 0° latitude, and the prime meridian is 0° longitude. The equator, which runs through the northern part of South America, divides Earth into the Northern **Hemisphere** and the Southern Hemisphere. Most of South America is in the Southern Hemisphere. The seasons of the Northern Hemisphere and the Southern Hemisphere are about six months apart. When it is winter in Chicago, a city in the Northern Hemisphere, it is summer in Lima, Peru, a city in the Southern Hemisphere.

SOUTH AMERICA: LANGMARKS

MAP KEY
SOUTH AMERICA: LANDMARKS

 Machu Picchu

 Lake Titicaca

 Angel Falls

 Aconcagua

 Perito Moreno Glacier

 Amazon Rain Forest

 Galápagos Islands

CARIBBEAN SEA

ATLANTIC OCEAN

EQUATOR

PACIFIC OCEAN

Longitude Lines

Latitude Lines

Cape Horn

SOUTH AMERICA
MERCATOR PROJECTION

0 km   500   1000   1500 km

scale at the Equator

GEOATLAS® - © 2001 Graphi-Ogre

South America's Andes Mountains make up the world's longest mountain chain at about 5,000 miles (8,047 km) long. The Andes run along South America's western side through Venezuela, Colombia, Ecuador, Peru, Bolivia, Chile, and Argentina. The highest peak in the Andes is Aconcagua, at 22,834 feet (6,960 m). Only Asia's Himalaya Mountains are higher than the Andes. East of the Andes lie the Guiana **Highlands** and the Brazilian Highlands, which are lower in **elevation** than the Andes. The Amazon **rain forest** lies in the plains of the Amazon Basin. At about 2 million square miles (5 million sq km) in area, the Amazon rain forest is Earth's largest **tropical** rain forest. It covers parts of Venezuela, Colombia, Ecuador, Peru, Brazil, and Bolivia. Running through part of the Amazon rain forest in Peru and Brazil is the Amazon River, which is Earth's second-longest river at 4,000 miles (6,437 km). Lake Titicaca, located between Bolivia and Peru, is 12,500 feet (3,810 m) above **sea level**. South America is also home to Angel Falls in Venezuela. At an elevation of 3,212 feet (979 m), it is the highest waterfall on Earth.

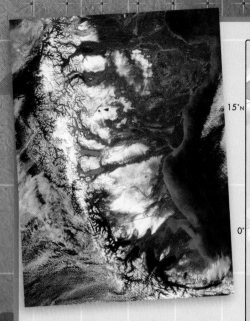

Clouds and snow cover most of the Andes in this photo, taken from space.

This photo, shot from space, shows the Amazon River and the Amazon rain forest.

SOUTH AMERICA: LAND AND WATER

Lake Marcaibo

Angel Falls

Guiana Highlands

Orinoco

Malpelo Island (COLOMBIA)

Llanos

Negro

Amazon

Marajó Island

EQUATOR

Amazon Basin

Amazon

Ucayali

Purus

Madeira

Tapajós

Xingu

Teles Pires

Tocantins

São Francisco

Andes

Mato Grosso Plateau

PACIFIC OCEAN

Lake Titicaca

Paraguay

Brazilian Highlands

Gran Chaco

Iguazú Falls

San Félix (CHILE)

San Ambrosio Island

ATLANTIC OCEAN

Atacama Desert

Paraná

Uruguay

Aconcagua

Pampas

Juan Fernández Islands (CHILE)

Río de la Plata

Colorado

Chiloé Island

Andes

Valdés Peninsula

Patagonia

Gulf of San Jorge

N

Falkland Islands (U.K.)

Strait of Magellan

Tierra del Fuego

South Georgia (U.K.)

Cape Horn

SOUTH AMERICA
MERCATOR PROJECTION

0 km   500   1000   1500 km

scale at the Equator

GEOATLAS® - © 2001 Graphi-Ogre

Countries of South America

The continent of South America consists of 12 independent countries. It also includes French Guiana, which belongs to France, and the Falkland Islands, which belong to the United Kingdom. Brazil is the largest country in South America at 3,284,426 square miles (8,506,624 sq km) in area. Brazil is larger than the United States, not including Alaska and Hawaii. More than 170 million people live in Brazil. In area, it is the fifth-largest country in the world. Suriname is South America's smallest country in area. It also has the lowest population. About 434,000 people live in its 63,251 square miles (163,819 sq km). Most of South America's countries were once ruled by Spain. In the early 1800s, eight South American countries gained their independence from Spain. During this time, Brazil gained its independence from Portugal, and Uruguay gained its independence from Brazil. In 1966, Guyana finally won its independence from the United Kingdom. The last South American country to gain independence was Suriname, which became free from the Netherlands in 1975.

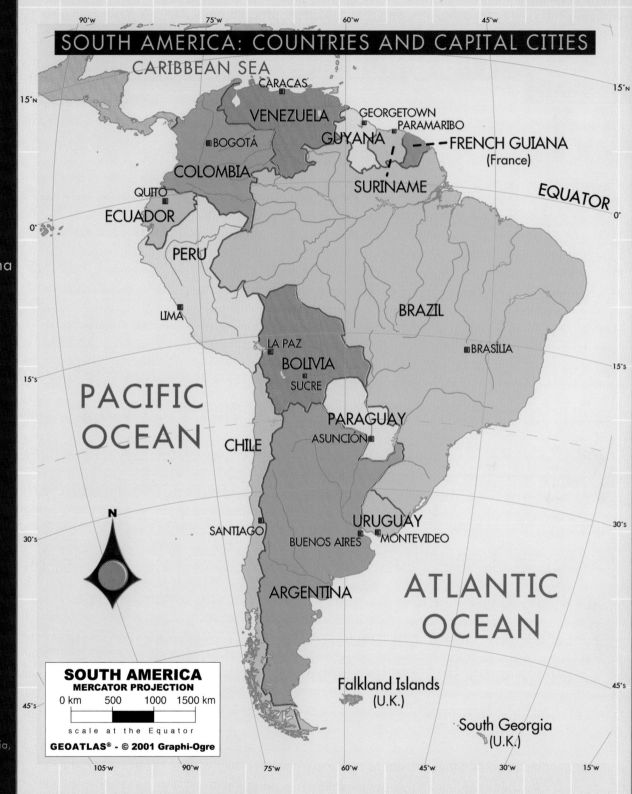

SOUTH AMERICA'S CAPITAL CITIES

■ Capital Cities

Lima, Peru
6,420,000

Santiago, Chile
4,250,000

Bogotá, Colombia
4,000,000

Buenos Aires, Argentina
3,000,000

Caracas, Venezuela
2,100,000

Brasília, Brazil
1,650,000

Montevideo, Uruguay
1,370,000

Quito, Ecuador
1,100,000

La Paz*, Bolivia
785,000

Asunción, Paraguay
560,000

Georgetown, Guyana
230,000

Paramaribo, Suriname
223,000

* La Paz is the actual capital of Bolivia,
where most government offices are
located. Sucre is the offical capital
where the Supreme Court meets.

SOUTH AMERICA: COUNTRIES AND CAPITAL CITIES

CARIBBEAN SEA

CARACAS

VENEZUELA

GEORGETOWN
PARAMARIBO

BOGOTÁ

GUYANA

FRENCH GUIANA
(France)

COLOMBIA

SURINAME

EQUATOR

QUITO

ECUADOR

PERU

BRAZIL

LIMA

LA PAZ

BRASÍLIA

BOLIVIA

SUCRE

PACIFIC
OCEAN

PARAGUAY

ASUNCIÓN

CHILE

URUGUAY

N

SANTIAGO

BUENOS AIRES

MONTEVIDEO

ARGENTINA

ATLANTIC
OCEAN

Falkland Islands
(U.K.)

South Georgia
(U.K.)

SOUTH AMERICA
MERCATOR PROJECTION

0 km   500   1000   1500 km

scale at the Equator

GEOATLAS® - © 2001 Graphi-Ogre

The Climate of South America

Most of South America has a tropical climate. Climate includes **temperature**, or how hot or cold a place is, and precipitation, or how much moisture falls from the sky. Much of South America receives plenty of rain. In places near the equator, daily rains help the Amazon rain forest to grow. Latitude also affects climate. Places closest to the equator are warm and wet. In the Amazon rain forest, temperatures average about 80°F (27°C), with rain averaging about 50 to 175 inches (127–445 cm) per year. In contrast to the Amazon rain forest, one of the driest places on Earth is the Atacama Desert in Chile and Peru, where rainfall is less than ½ inch (1 cm) per year. It does not rain very much because of the Peru Current, a cold Pacific Ocean current that cools the air. Little precipitation falls along the coast because cold air doesn't hold as much moisture as warm air. Places along the coast where the Peru Current flows also have colder temperatures than other coasts at the same latitude.

Caribbean Sea

Equator

Pacific Ocean

Atlantic Ocean

CLIMATE

Tropical Wet

Tropical Dry

Semiarid

Arid

Mediterranean

Highlands

Marine West Coast

Humid Subtropical

South America's Plants and Animals

Plants and animals live in all parts of South America. Many plants and animals living in the Amazon rain forest may not have been identified by people yet. The sloth lives in the trees of the forest and is found only in **Central America** and South America. The capybara, Earth's largest **rodent** at 4 feet (1 m) long, looks like a large pig with fur. It also lives in the rain forest. Colorful birds, including toucans and parrots, fly among the trees. The anaconda, one of Earth's largest snakes at 30 feet (9 m) long, can also be found in the rain forest. Plant-eating manatees, also called sea cows, swim in the Amazon River as do fierce, meat-eating piranha fish. Air plants, which grow on other plants but get most of their water and food from the air, grow in the treetops of the Amazon rain forest. Air plants include Spanish moss and the spider orchid, a beautiful flower. Trees growing in the rain forest include Brazil nut trees, rubber trees, and cacao trees, which grow beans used to make chocolate and cocoa.

Clockwise from the top right: *This black spider monkey can hang by his tail. The llama is the "camel" of the Andes mountains. The giant sea turtles of Ecuador's Galápagos Islands can weigh more than 500 pounds (227 kg). These wild orchids grow near the ruins of Machu Picchu, an ancient Incan city.*

90°w 75°w 60°w 45°w

VENEZUELA
GUYANA   FRENCH GUIANA
COLOMBIA   SURINAME
ECUADOR   EQUATOR
PERU
                    BRAZIL
15°s   BOLIVIA
            PARAGUAY
        CHILE
                URUGUAY
30°s
            ARGENTINA

PACIFIC
OCEAN
45°s
                ATLANTIC OCEAN

105°w 90°w 75°w 60°w 45°w 30°w 15°w

Making a Living in South America

Many large farms in South America hire workers to harvest crops including bananas, coffee, and sugar, which are **exported** to countries around the world. Farmers also raise sheep for wool. Some South Americans work in the mining **industry**. Venezuela produces the most oil in South America. Colombia leads the world in mining emeralds, a valuable green **gemstone**. Chile has Earth's only known source of sodium nitrate, which is found in the Atacama Desert. This **mineral** is used in **fertilizer**, which helps plants to grow. Anchovetas, jack mackerel, and sardines are fish caught off the coast of Chile. Chile and Peru both have large fishing industries. Brazil leads South America in forest products that include rubber, wood, medicines, oils, and waxes made from trees. Coconuts, brazil nuts, and dates are also harvested from trees that grow in the rain forest. Most South American countries manufacture cloth, food, and shoes. Argentina, Brazil, Chile, and Ecuador make and sell cars, airplanes, and televisions. About half of the people in South America work in banking, health care, **transportation**, and **communication**.

BRAZIL

Atlantic Ocean

This factory worker in Brazil is putting together parts of an airplane.

Cayambe .

ECUADOR

Pacific Ocean

These farmers are harvesting barley in a field near the Cayambe volcano, in Ecuador.

CHILE

Santiago .

Pacific Ocean

A young artist in Santiago, Chile, is working on a painting that will be shown in Santiago's Palace of Fine Arts.

The People of South America

Scientists believe that the first people who lived in South America came from Asia about 15,000 years ago. From the 1200s to the 1500s, the Inca, a Native American group, built an important civilization in South America. In 1535, they were conquered by Spanish explorers. European settlers fought Native Americans for land and riches. Many Native Americans died from fighting and from European **diseases**. Europeans tried to force Native Americans to work on huge farms and in mines. However, Africans were brought to South America to work as slaves. In the early 1800s, Spanish colonies in South America gained freedom from Spain, and most made slavery against the law. Later, Europeans from France, Great Britain, Italy, the Netherlands, and Poland moved to South America. Today many South Americans have **ancestors** who are Native American and European, African and European, or Native American and African. Most South Americans speak Spanish because the continent was ruled by the Spanish. Many other languages are spoken there, as well.

Barranquilla

COLOMBIA

Pacific Ocean

This girl takes a rest after dancing in a parade in Barranquilla, Colombia.

Quito ◼
ECUADOR

Pacific Ocean

These boys live and play in the city of Quito, Ecuador.

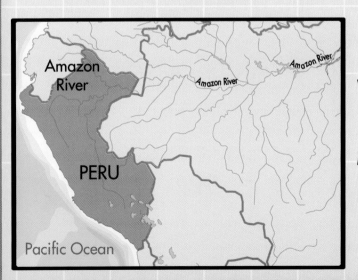

Amazon River

Amazon River

Amazon River

PERU

Pacific Ocean

These women live in Peru. They are paddling a canoe on the Amazon River.

A Scientist in South America

Peruvian Guillermo Cock is a South American **archaeologist** who studies **cultures** of peoples of the Andes. From 1999 to 2001, Cock worked in a poor town called Tupac Amaru, outside of Lima, Peru. In this place was an area where ancient Incan people were buried, called Puruchuco-Huaquerones. At Puruchuco-Huaquerones, Cock and the other archaeologists found more than 2,200 **mummies** buried with items such as **pottery** and cloths. The mummies included children, men, and women from different social classes who died from many different causes. By studying these 500-year-old mummies, scientists can piece together details, such as how the Inca lived, their health, and their roles in society. Cock and the other archaeologists found that almost half of the mummies were children under the age of 12. Scientists believe that many of the children died from **infections** or from anemia, a blood disease. Cock shares his findings with other scientists by writing about them in books and magazines. He also shares information with museums that have exhibits about cultures of the Andes.

Glossary

ancestors (AN-ses-terz) Relatives who lived long ago.

archaeologist (ar-kee-AH-luh-jist) Someone who studies the remains of people to see how they lived.

Central America (SEN-trul uh-MER-ih-kuh) The southern part of North America.

communication (kuh-myoo-nih-KAY-shun) The sharing of facts or feelings.

cultures (KUL-churz) The beliefs, practices, and arts of different groups of people.

diseases (duh-ZEEZ-ez) Illnesses or sicknesses.

earthquakes (URTH-kwayks) Shakings of Earth's surface caused by the movement of large pieces of land, called plates, that run into each other.

elevation (eh-luh-VAY-shun) The heights of objects.

era (ER-uh) A period of time or history.

exported (EK-sport-ed) Sent to another place or land to be sold.

fertilizer (FUR-til-eye-zer) A substance put in soil to help crops grow.

gemstone (JEM-stohn) A precious stone, such as a diamond or ruby.

hemisphere (HEH-muh-sfeer) One half of Earth or another sphere.

highlands (HY-lindz) Areas with many hills or mountains.

industry (IN-dus-tree) A moneymaking business in which many people work to produce a particular product.

infections (in-FEK-shunz) Sicknesses caused by germs.

mineral (MIH-ner-ul) A natural element that is not an animal, a plant, or another living thing.

mummies (MUH-meez) Dead bodies that have been kept from rotting.

pottery (PAH-tuh-ree) Pots, vases, and similar objects made of clay.

rain forest (RAYN FOR-est) A thick forest that receives a large amount of rain during the year.

rodent (ROH-dent) An animal with gnawing teeth, such as a mouse.

sea level (SEE LEH-vul) The height of the top of the ocean.

symbols (SIM-bulz) Objects or pictures that stand for something else.

temperature (TEM-pruh-cher) How hot or cold something is.

transportation (tranz-per-TAY-shun) A way of traveling from one place to another.

tropical (TRAH-puh-kul) Warm year-round.

Index

Web Sites

Due to the changing nature of Internet links, PowerKids Press has developed an online list of Web sites related to the subject of this book. This site is updated regularly. Please use this link to access the list:

www.powerkidslinks.com/asc/samerica/